P9-DMU-963

Also by Thomas P. McElroy, Jr.

The New Handbook of Attracting Birds

THE HABITAT GUIDE TO BIRDING

Illustrated by Matthew Kalmenoff

NLB

Nick Lyons Books

THE HABITAT GUIDE TO BIRDING

Thomas P. McElroy, Jr.

Copyright © 1974 by Thomas P. McElroy, Jr.

ALL RIGHTS RESERVED. No part of this book may be reproduced in any manner without the express written consent of the publisher, except in the case of brief excerpts in critical reviews and articles. All inquiries should be addressed to: Nick Lyons Books, 31 West 21 Street, New York, NY 10010.

Printed in the United States of America

10   9   8   7   6   5   4   3   2   1

Published by arrangement with Alfred A. Knopf, Inc.

Library of Congress Cataloging-in-Publication Data

McElroy, Thomas P., 1914–
  The habitat guide to birding.

  Reprint. Originally published: New York : Knopf, 1974.
  Bibliography: p.
  Includes index.
  1. Bird watching—United States.   2. Birds—United States—Habitat.   I. Title.
QL682.M33   1987   598'.07'23473   87-4034
ISBN 0-9431130-36-3

To Tommy and Wendy

*and grandchildren everywhere, with
the hope that they, too, may
thrill to the flight of the eagle,
know the beauty of the cardinal,
and revere the cathedral tones
of the wood thrush.*

Note:

Since the original publication of *The Habitat Guide,* the names of some of the birds listed on the American Ornithologist's Union checklist have changed. A table of the changes appears below.

NAME AS USED IN BOOK	CORRECTED NAME
Caracara	Caracara, Crested
Cardinal	Cardinal, Northern
Catbird	Catbird, Gray
Crow, Common	Crow, American
Dove, Ground	Ground-Dove, Common
Duck, Black	Duck, American Black
Duck, Fulvous Tree	Whistling-Duck, Fulvous
Egret, Common	Egret, Great
Flicker, Yellow-shafted	Flicker, Northern
Flycatcher, Trail's	Flycatcher, Alder
Gallinule, Common	Moorhen, Common
Gannet	Gannet, Northern
Goshawk	Goshawk, Northern
Hawk, Duck	Falcon, Peregrine
Hawk, Marsh	Harrier, Northern
Hawk, Pigeon	Merlin
Heron, Great White	Heron, Great Blue
Heron Green	Heron, Green-backed
Heron, Louisiana	Heron, Tricolored
Ibis, Wood	Stork, Wood
Junco, Oregon	Junco, Dark-eyed
Junco, Slate-colored	Junco, Dark-eyed
Kite, Everglade	Kite, Snail
Knot	Knot, Red
Mockingbird	Mockingbird, Northern
Oriole, Baltimore	Oriole, Northern
Oriole, Spotted-breasted	Oriole, Spot-breasted
Owl, Barn	Barn-Owl, Northern
Hawk-Owl	Hawk-Owl, Northern
Owl, Saw-whet	Owl, Northern Saw-whet
Owl, Screech	Screech-Owl, Eastern
Pelican, White	Pelican, American White
Pewee, Eastern Wood	Wood-Pewee, Eastern
Pintail	Pintail, Northern
Plover, Upland	Sandpiper, Upland
Puffin, Common	Puffin, Atlantic
Quail, Bobwhite	Bobwhite, Northern
Robin	Robin, American
Scoter, Common	Scoter, Black
Skylark, European	Skylark, Eurasian
Sparrow, Cape Sable	Sparrow, Seaside
Sparrow, Dusky Seaside	Sparrow, Seaside
Sparrow, Ipswich	Sparrow, Savannah
Sparrow, Tree	Sparrow, American Tree
Starling	Starling, European
Swallow, Rough-winged	Swallow, Northern Rough-winged
Swan, Whistling	Swan, Tundra
Tern, Noddy	Noddy, Brown
Warbler, Myrtle	Warbler, Yellow-rumped
Warbler, Parula	Parula, Northern
Woodpecker, Northern Three-toed	Woodpecker, Three-toed
Wren, Long-billed Marsh	Wren, Marsh
Wren, Short-billed Marsh	Wren, Sedge
Warbler, Yellowthroat	Yellowthroat, Common
Widgeon, European	Widgeon, Eurasian

Contents

A Guide
to the Habitat Lists

A Guide
to the Illustrations

Preface

The sudden realization that man is inherently dependent upon the related functions of the natural community has, in part, initiated a great resurgence of interest in all outdoor activities. People are searching for fundamental truths—the basic laws of survival and their meanings in terms of human welfare and happiness. Some seek answers in the remoteness of the backcountry; others must challenge the beckoning peaks of high mountains; and others find a degree of solitude in plying wilderness waterways. But for many, the most meaningful rewards are found in following the lives of birds, for birds have represented the enduring qualities of life since eons past.

Although I have been interested in birds since childhood, I must admit that I find it somewhat difficult to pinpoint those qualities which sustained my interest over so long a period. Perhaps I was content, in those formative years, to add a "new" bird to my list, to know where the oriole or kingbird nested, to thrill at the swift flight of a hunting hawk, and to find solace in the bell-like tones of the thrushes as I returned from my woodland wanderings. The birds were there, and I was content to have them as my daily companions.

Even in this most casual form of acceptance, bird watching was a deeply satisfying experience. In more recent years, however, I have become increasingly aware of more significant attributes to be found in observing wild birds in their natural habitats. Also, the dimension of concern has been added; birds are recognized as the earliest and truest indicators of environmental change. I am not alone in these discoveries, for there is a growing human force, informed and inquisitive, whose intellect cannot be satisfied by the mere facts of existence alone. This is especially true relative to the comparatively new science of ecology. Where the relationships of life and environment are involved, this new force demands positive answers. In the case of bird watching, it is no longer sufficient to say the wood thrush is a brown speckled bird of the forest. Why is it there? How does it survive? What does it contribute to the total forest community? The answers to such indicative questions carry the bird watcher beyond the staid practice of merely listing recognized species.

Recognizing these facts, this book, then, is manifold in purpose. Primarily, its intent is to improve one's skill and to increase one's pleasure as a birder. The pursuit of these objectives is through an innovative approach to the whole field of bird watching: that birders can be helped in locating, identifying, and understanding birds through a knowledge of their physical adaptations and behavioral patterns as associated with the habitats in which they live. Also, this book is based on the premise that birds are an important functional unit in the total natural community, and that through the understanding of these functions and the community, the birder can pursue his interests with a keener knowledge and find greater personal rewards.

This book also recognizes the hypothesis that one or more species of birds can be found in every conceivable type of habitat, no matter how specific we may be in designating the habitat's scientific nomenclature, or how careful we are in delineating its boundaries. Birds are everywhere, and this fact alone injects the element of evolutionary mystery and provides innumerable ecological equations to challenge the most curious of intellects.

From this myriad of adaptations, relationships, and similar habitat characteristics, I have fashioned the basis for this book.

Birds are not distributed uniformly throughout any geographical area. Each species survives best in a certain type of habitat because of adaptations and specialization by generations of its ancestors. Habitats differ greatly in their biological and physical characteristics. Some support large numbers of a few species; others sustain lesser numbers of a greater variety. Recognizing these differences in representative habitats of the eastern half of our continent, from the tundra to the semitropics, it soon becomes evident that the techniques of locating, observing, and identifying birds will vary somewhat from one habitat to another. Also, the kinds of preferred clothing and equipment for watchers will differ as they progress from forests to marshlands to seashores. In chapters pertaining to specific habitats, I have included certain field techniques (including the use of equipment) that will make birding in each area an enjoyable and rewarding experience. In addition, I have devoted an entire chapter to field techniques in general, and another to the important matter of selecting and using binoculars and scopes. The beginning bird watcher may wish to read these two chapters (16 and 17) before going on to the rest of the book.

And in the preparation of this book I have not neglected the aesthetic appeal of bird watching, for it is this emotional quality that lures most of us afield.

Mostly, this book has grown from my many years of watching birds, and from my keen interest in the ecology of our land. But I hasten to acknowledge those whose work has made bird watching such an easy pursuit to follow. Generations of scientists have given us a system of organization —a scientific classification and nomenclature for birds of the world. Men such as Edward H. Forbush, Frank M. Chapman, Arthur Cleveland Bent, and Alexander Sprunt, Jr. have given us detailed life histories; Andrew J. Berger, Josselyn Van Tyne, and Olin S. Pettingill, Jr. have developed comprehensive courses of study for the serious student; and Roger Tory Peterson, Richard H. Pough, and others have simplified the task of bird identification. And in a book of this kind, one cannot ignore the efforts of Eugene P. Odum, R. F. Daubenmire, Henry J. Oosting, Paul B. Sears, and other pioneering ecologists.

This book is largely a personal effort, but I am especially grateful to Olin S. Pettingill, Jr., Director of the Laboratory of Ornithology, Cornell University, for his interest and suggestions for certain portions of the text; to Paul Knoop, director of the Aullwood Audubon Center at Dayton, Ohio, for his time afield with me; and to Hannah H. McElroy for many months of patience and understanding. But mostly, I am indebted to Blanche E. Getchen for many hours of assistance in preparation of the final text, and to my editor, Angus Cameron, for his continued guidance, inspiration, and enduring patience.

T . P . M .

Suggestions for Using This Book

Birders are individualists, and their personal interests are quite diversified. Consequently, there is no singular technique or method of procedure for using this book. Its organization and content are such that it will be a source of help to the amateur and the experienced birder alike. The following notes and suggestions will explain the book's features and make it easier to use in the pursuit of personal objectives.

- The habitats included here were chosen because of their dominance in the eastern half of our continent and for their attractiveness to birds. They are grouped in a manner convenient to the bird watcher—what you may view from one place, or on one field trip.
- The names used in the text are from the *American Ornithologists' Union's Check-List of North American Birds*, 5th edition, 1957. For clarity and ease of use, in any extensive lists, birds are listed alphabetically, first by families (common names) and then by species. In most cases, the family headings include only those genera which are represented by one or more species in the list. For example, the family of "Crows, Magpies, and Jays" may be listed as "Jays" and followed by the species "Blue."
- Scientific names have been purposely avoided in most cases, and are used only where necessary for clarity.
- Birds described for identification (field marks, etc.) are males in spring plumage unless indicated otherwise.

• For information on a specific species, use the index. Often, the same species is referred to in several habitats. Details of characteristics and habits will be found in the most appropriate section of the text.

• The numerous illustrations in the margins are intended to be both atmospheric and informative. Mostly, they are applicable to the immediately adjacent text.

• You will soon become aware that this is not a complete treatise on bird identification. It is not intended to be, for this subject has been covered expertly by others. However, you will find information on methods of identification, and in some instances, field marks and characteristic habits will be pointed out as a means of applying these methods. This book will supplement your favorite field guide.

• Study the appropriate section when planning a field trip to a particular type of habitat. It will help you to know what birds to expect and what behavioral patterns to look for when studying various species. Also, this book will serve as a guide to the selection of habitats for locating specific species.

• Use this book as a follow-up to field trips and as a cross-check for notes taken in the field. Make this a personal book; additional border sketches and notes will enhance its personal value.

• Many of you may find this book an introduction to the ecology of bird communities. And so it was intended, for we cannot really know birds without understanding the environment in which they live.

THE HABITAT GUIDE TO BIRDING

Birds are an integral part of the American landscape, and their numbers and kinds vary as the landscape varies. Our lofty mountains with their adjacent rolling hills, our wide valleys with their meandering rivers, grasslands, and fields of grain, our sculptured coastlines and sandy beaches—it is to these panoramic wonders that birds add color, song, movement, and, above all else, life itself. The cry of sea birds along New England's coastline, the clatter of wintering geese on the back bays of Virginia's lowlands, the statuesque herons and egrets atop the cypress and the mangroves, the raucous call of crows above an Ohio cornfield—these things are as symbolically Americana as the physical terrain upon which they dwell.

America is especially blessed with birds, both in numbers and in varieties. Mostly, this population is not a static one, but one that changes with the seasons and with the environment.

As the cold days of winter settle upon the land, the song sparrows, catbirds, and towhees give way to the white-throats and juncos. The field sparrows and bobolinks no longer feed upon the seed heads of foxtail and bluestem grasses; in their stead, we hear the tinkling of tree sparrows and redpolls. The daily preachings of the red-eyed vireo no longer resound from his woodland pulpit. The bluebirds (except the pair in the sumacs) have gone. The nest in the box elder is wind-blown and deserted; but the tree's winged seeds, hard-fast to the supple twigs, rustle

1 In Search of Birds

their defiance at the winter winds. Their fate is sustenance for evening grosbeaks and purple finches. Only now, in the quiet bleakness of winter, can we hope to see the snowy owl, or his miniature counterpart, the saw-whet.

Springtime brings a change in mood and tempo. Life is breathed into the earth once again, and it responds with a crescendo of song and the beat of birds on the wing.

All movement is northward. Flocks of tree swallows swirl in cyclonic fashion as they leave the sedges and shrubs where they roosted for the night. Gradually the flocks thin, and flight is resumed; they will feed as they travel. Waves of warblers progress from treetop to treetop as they rest and feed; their long flight will be resumed in the darkness of night. Everywhere, all across the land, birds are on the move, and the tide rolls ever northward.

In the fall, this great tide reverses itself; the flow of life is southward. The sandy spits along our sea beaches overflow with migrating shore birds. Thousands of ducks leave the sloughs and potholes of the Midwest and prairie provinces of Canada. And the warblers—their thin lisps in the stillness of the night reveal their myriad numbers—are on the wing again. But come the dawn and daylight hours, they can be seen flitting about the treetops in search of insects to replenish their energy for the coming night's long journey.

But it is during the warming months of summer, when birds are at home, that we can observe the excitement of their living. All activities seem to take on a hastening pace; there is so much to be done before chill winds once again force the departure of most species. For some, there is no need to hurry. The red-bellied woodpecker can spend days drilling his hole in the hard dry stub of a pine; he will not move with the cold. The goldfinches can remain in their social flocks; the milkweed pods will not release their down and seeds until early July. But for those who will leave in the fall, time is of the essence. There is territorial homesteading to be done, and a mate to be found. Hours will be spent in singing and warding off intruders. A hundred searching trips or more must be made to find appropriate nesting materials. Eggs must be laid and brooded, and thousands more forays made in search of food. The young must be taught to fend for themselves, and then, only then, may the pace of living be slowed. And slow it does, for there is a mysterious quiet about the sun-baked gardens and woodlands during the hot days of late summer. Old Red-eye now preaches to an unresponsive congregation.

Environmental changes also help keep much of our bird population in a state of fluctuation. Natural succession is slow, but nevertheless effective. A pond in the open, edged mainly with water lilies, may appeal to the pied-billed grebe and a few dabbling ducks. As grasses, sedges, cattails, and loosestrife begin to dominate the edges, these few species will be joined by others such as red-winged blackbirds, swamp sparrows, marsh wrens, and Virginia rails. The appearance of shrubs—willows, black alders, and buttonbush—will bring yellowthroats, song sparrows, catbirds, yellow warblers, and other shrub-loving species. If this natural succession were allowed to continue undisturbed, the forest would eventually be the permanent habitat of the pond's borders. Birds of the previous pond-edge communities would be gone; chickadees, titmice, vireos, nuthatches, ovenbirds, woodpeckers, and other woodland birds would be dominant.

When man enters the scene with his monstrous machines, environmental changes are apt to be radical. With a few swipes by a bulldozer or backhoe, a sand spit, a marsh, or a fencerow can disappear from the face of the earth. The sad part of such intrusions is this: there is little recuperative power in a habitat of concrete and steel.

But change is the essence of bird watching's appeal. From season to season, from mountain to valley, from field to forest, no matter when or where you go, there is a constant newness each time you are afield. Each type of habitat supports a different variety of birds. Birding knows no season, requires no license, and is of interest to all age groups. Birds belong to us all—free for the watching.

We think of a bird's habitat as being the place or particular type of area in which it has a habit of living. Actually, it is much more than that; it is a combination of interacting physical and biological (community) factors

that produce an environment to which an individual species has become best adapted through innumerable generations. Each species remains in, or returns to, the type of habitat in which it was born. Although a certain habitat is often home to a variety of birds, we speak of each species as being best suited, and adapted to, a specific habitat. When all plants and animals within a given area are considered, we refer to the area as a community.

Most species of birds are so instinctively bound and so physiologically adapted to one type of habitat that they cannot tolerate environmental changes, nor can they survive by moving to a totally different habitat. Other species, however, are ecologically tolerant in varying degrees. In my home state of Florida, the Everglade kite faces possible extinction because of its complete dependence on a delicately balanced fresh-water habitat. It feeds exclusively on the fresh-water *Pomacea*. This snail breeds and thrives in the flooded shallows of the Glades. But man has entered the scene. Hundreds of miles of straight-line drainage ditches (ostensibly for flood control) and the indiscriminate use of pesticides have narrowed the habitat in which the snails and the kites can survive. By contrast, the robin is a most tolerant species; its food habits are not so specialized. I have seen it nest in the gardens and parks of the Carolinas, along the shrubby fencerows and woodland borders of New England, and in the openings of Quebec's northernmost forests. Still other species have a moderate tolerance for environmental changes. If we are to know where to find and watch birds, we should have a knowledge of these tolerances and of the dominating forces within the bird community. Why are the birds there? What attracts them? What are the relationships between species and selected home sites? An understanding of the functions within the bird community will make our trips afield more successful and more meaningful.

The bobolink returns to its home in a Wisconsin hayfield. It welcomes spring from the bobbing tip of a dried goldenrod stem, its song bubbling forth in a series of alternating high and low metallic notes. The wood thrush announces its homecoming from the deep shade of a Pennsylvania forest with a song of the flute—clear, mellow, and ending with a vibrato that fades into the shadowy depths. The American bittern claims its territory by "driving stakes" along the marshy borders of a remote lake in Maine. Everywhere across the land, birds return home in the spring to a particular biological niche in the outdoor community.

The bobolink may return to the very field in which it was hatched slightly less than a year ago. It does this not by choice, or by any calculated evaluation, but by instinct alone. The young bobolink is the culmination of all the inherited reflexes, responses, habits, and abilities of its parents and countless generations of its ancestors. Have they not made the great flight down the east coast of our continent and across the Bahamas to Jamaica? And then another five hundred miles across an islandless ocean to the shores of South America? Have they not spent a hundred thousand winters on the pampas of Argentina? Have they not returned to sing from a hundred thousand golden-rod stems? Have they not known fear at the screaming of a hawk, or the quiet passing of a fox?

Yes. All the experiences of living to be encountered by the young bobolink have been known countless times before. But unknowingly, and in an infinitesimal way, it will contribute to the inheritance that will assure the survival of future generations.

The wood thrush senses security in the cool shade of the forest. Its large eyes have developed a special keenness in the subdued light; it avoids the bright sunshine. It experiences little competition as it forages about the forest floor, flipping dead leaves aside with its bill, seeking crickets, grubs, spiders, ants, flies, and earthworms. Most of its woodland neighbors either are seed eaters or catch their insects at higher levels. The wood thrush is an understory specialist—it feeds low, perches low, and nests low. And always, its tawny back blends with the protective browns of the forest floor. Just as were its progenitors throughout the eons, it is a creature of the forest community. It takes, it gives, and it survives.

And the bittern, has it not always known the wetness of the marsh? Over the great span of time past, it has been so much a part of this wetland habitat that the striations of its plumage now mimic the reeds and grasses in which it lives. Unlike most herons, its way of life is solitary and secretive; it does not feed in flocks, nor does it colonize for nesting. It is a loner—a master of stealth and concealment.

And so it is with the ducks and the geese, with the hawks and the falcons, and with the warblers and the sparrows. And so it is with the plovers and the sandpipers, and with the terns and the gulls. Each species instinctively fulfills its destiny as an active member of the particular community to which it is irrevocably bound.

The Outdoor Community

To the human eye, the outdoor community in which birds live presents a deceptive façade of harmony and tranquillity. In reality, it is a composite of dynamic forces that function interdependently in the never-ending struggle for survival. It is not unlike the community in which man himself lives; it has its basement dwellers, street-level residents, and high-rise occupants; it has its own factories, shopping centers, police force, garbage collectors, robbers, and parasitic welfare cases. The community functions as a circuitous chain of events propelled by the energies of birth, competition, and death. The green leaves that have survived the competition for sunlight and are structured by the carbon they have taken from the air may satiate the appetite of a ravenous caterpillar; the life juices of the caterpillar may flow in the bloodstream of a newly hatched cuckoo; the cuckoo may strengthen the sharp-shinned hawk who, through his own demise, will eventually release the carbon for use by other green plants. Life within the community beats with a fundamental rhythm of natural laws. Birds are an essential part of this rhythmic beat.

There are numerous and varied physical and biological factors associated with each type of bird community that largely determine the numbers and varieties of species it can support. These factors, when divided into their innumerable components, associations, and relationships, form the basis for detailed ecological studies. Obviously, that is not the purpose of this book, but we should be concerned with the major and more recognizable factors of community structure. This will help us determine where we have the best chance of finding certain species and give us a working knowledge of what species we can expect to find in a particular habitat.

Plants—not birds or other animals—are the structural backbone of the community. Either directly or indirectly, they are the source of all energy necessary to maintain the lives of all organisms. In most communities, they provide food, home sites, and protective cover. From the minutest plankton to the most stalwart of trees, all plants are in some way involved in maintaining the rhythmic beat of life within the community. Plant growth, as we know, is subject to such climatic and ecological conditions as air temperature, precipitation, humidity, exposure, wind, light intensity, and soil composition. Plant groups that tolerate these conditions in various combinations determine the numbers and species of birds a particular community will attract and support. When a degree of uniformity is reached through a certain combination of these conditions, a corresponding degree of uniformity is reached in the plant life and in the animal life. These factors, along with topography and geographical location, constitute the basis for a specific type of habitat. These principles apply in both terrestrial and aquatic communities.

The importance and contributions of birds to a balanced environment are difficult to evaluate. Their associations with other animal and plant members of the community are so numerous and often so obscure, but nevertheless important, that ecologists may never unravel all the ramifications involved. However, we do know enough about these relationships to realize that birds are a significant part of the intricate web of all living things, including man. We know, for example, that such species as the bobolink, field sparrow, and junco consume tons of weed seeds every year. As far as community balance is concerned, the amount of seeds actually consumed has less significance than the thinning out and distribution of the various plant species from which they came.

In a forest, an elm tree succumbs to disease and the shade of a beech-maple canopy. Woodpeckers chip away

the bark in search of grubs and insects; they drill nesting cavities in the softer limbs and trunk areas. In doing so, they hasten the processes that will eventually return the tree to the soil. A limb breaks at a weakened spot and falls; rain water fills the cavities and helps the process of rotting; eventually, a wind storm tumbles the tree to the ground. Here it may serve as a drumming log for the ruffed grouse, or it may provide a temporary home for a chipmunk or a deer mouse. But now the bacteria and fungi take over, and gradually the elm is returned to the soil, releasing its carbon and other elements to be used once again.

Birds might be looked upon as the "middlemen" in the community's pyramid of numbers. Certain songbirds may rear a dozen or more young in a season, but the seeds, insects, and smaller animals upon which they feed are produced in tremendous numbers. Along with weather, disease, and other natural deterrents, birds act as a "lid" over these exploding populations. Vertebrates higher up on the pyramid aid in the same repressive controls over the songbird population through predation. Species such as vultures, crows, and gulls serve as community scavengers.

Aquatic communities tend to be less stable and not as easily defined as the terrestrial varieties. Nevertheless, the same ecological principles govern the survival of species, and birds are involved in many ways. A duck flying from one pond to another may carry a number of tiny floating duckweed plants on its body. In doing so it helps distribute and perpetuate its own food supply. A bittern feeding in the marsh may spear a minnow infested with tiny parasitic grubs, some of which will remain, live, and lay eggs within the bittern's mouth. As the bittern feeds, the eggs are washed into the water, where they hatch, feed, and eventually infest another minnow, thus continuing an intricate aquatic life cycle.

By now we know our bird population is widely distributed among a variety of habitats. We also know that feeding habits, nesting requirements, physiological adaptations, and other factors tend to limit many species to a certain type of habitat. This is especially true during the nesting season. During migration, when birds are concerned chiefly with travel routes, feeding, and resting, they can often be observed outside their normal nesting areas. Also, we should remember that the more pronounced natural communities seldom have definitive boundaries; more often than not, there is a transition zone (known as an *ecotone*) from one community to another. These ecotones often support more numbers and more species of birds than either adjacent community. For example, the transition zone between an uncultivated field and a hardwood forest may consist of the hardier field plants, a variety of shrubs and vines, and a number of young encroachment trees from the forest. This mixture of vegetation provides an abundance and variety of foods, nesting sites, and protective cover. In the eastern part of our country, this type of ecotone would attract such species as the field sparrow, song sparrow, cardinal, catbird, brown thrasher, yellow-breasted chat, rufous-sided towhee, indigo bunting, prairie warbler, and chestnut-sided warbler.

It now becomes quite obvious: the greater the variety of habitats we visit, the greater the variety of birds we can expect to find.

2 Habitats and Bird Identification

One or more species of birds are indigenous to every type of habitat on planet Earth, with the possible exception of some remote interior areas of Antarctica. And each biological niche within the larger habitats or communities supports a number of birds that have become adapted to its peculiar physical and biological characteristics. To understand why this is so, we must reach back into prehistoric times.

Scientists have proved beyond doubt that birds are descendants of the early reptiles. The skeletal forms of present-day birds and the fossilized remains traceable to intermittent periods are the basis of their proof. But why, how, and when these reptiles took to the air is speculated upon with a lesser degree of certainty. The most acceptable hypothesis is that certain reptiles first took to the trees because of competition for food and living space, and for their own safety. Then, over a period of millions of years, the physical adaptations that permitted jumping, gliding, and flight ensued in progressive order.

The oldest known bird fossil, *Archaeopteryx*, was found in a stratum of Upper Jurassic rock dating back some 140 million years. But the next fossil of record came from a stratum formed millions of years later. By the Eocene epoch, some 50 million years ago, the physical characteristics of birds approached their present form. Also, during this period, they probably made their most rapid advances in the processes of evolution.

One can only speculate on the number of birds in the past. All scientific evidence indicates there were greater numbers of species and individuals than presently exist. As the dinosaurs and other giant reptiles disappeared, the environment favored greater safety and proliferation of avian species. In addition, great physical changes on the surface of the earth produced new and varied habitats. Mountains were formed, islands rose from the sea, and great forests appeared but gave way to the grassland of the drier leeward side of the mountains. Birds radiated into the new habitats wrought by such cataclysmic changes. Not until the era of glaciers changed the relative uniformity of climate did birds suffer any drastic losses in the proliferation of species. The advance and retreat of glaciers is credited with starting the vast north and south movement of birds that is inherent in the migratory patterns of today.

Most species were limited to a specific range by such factors as the availability of food and cover, physical barriers, and climatic changes, and by their own adaptation to a specific type of environment. Woodlands, grasslands, and extensive marshes barred the natural distribution of species, even though comparable habitats may have existed beyond their distant boundaries. Some species were tolerant of greater temperature extremes than were others; some needed the longest of days in order to find sufficient food; and others needed consistent winds and thermals for prolonged flight.

As birds filled the various habitats, their tremendous numbers pressured the need for continued adaptation and specialization. In the forest, for example, different species occupy varying levels from the ground to the treetops. In the wetlands, we find waders, probers, skimmers, divers, dabblers, and other specialists. By selection (or perhaps by population pressures) each species has become adapted to the means of survival within a particular niche of each habitat. The physical features and characteristic habits, which developed over the eons and are needed to ensure this survival, are pronounced and visible; thus, they are a definite aid to bird identification.

The fact that birds do occupy every conceivable type

of biological niche, and that their kinds vary with each, makes bird watching an intriguing activity, and identification its most challenging objective. Recognition becomes the key to gratification.

Today, bird identification is comparatively easy, for the basic research has been done, and the results are available in compact field guides, thousands of photographs, and many excellent recordings. Every species indigenous to our continent is included in the recent field guides, and most of their songs are recorded for public use. In this chapter, and throughout this book, we are concerned mainly with identification as it relates to habits and habitat associations. Some emphasis is placed on the use of field marks, and on the recognition of songs and calls.* Following are some guides for recognizing birds by their location.

Birds on the Ground

Many birds spend a considerable amount of time on the ground, but here the mannerisms of various species are often quite different. The robin hops and runs across the lawn, stops suddenly, and cocks its head slightly to the side, watching for the slightest movement of a grub or earthworm. The grackle walks with a deliberate stride, but the mourning dove sort of "patters" along with short steps, bobbing its head back and forth as it goes. The ovenbird walks ever so quietly across the forest floor, its tail perked at a jaunty angle and flipping a bit with each step, but jays and sparrows travel on the ground by hopping. The sparrowlike water pipit walks, but it can be recognized by the constant bobbing of its white-edged tail and by its slender bill. Spotted sandpipers and waterthrushes also walk, but they "teeter" as though they were overweight in the front.

Woodland thrushes search for food by flipping leaves aside with their bills, but towhees and fox sparrows can be heard scratching amid the dry leaves of the forest floor. They do not scratch like a chicken, but hop back and forth, kicking the leaves aside with both feet.

* Additional information on bird identification will be found in succeeding chapters and in the Bibliography.

Some ground-feeding (or near-ground) species give clues to their identity by traveling in flocks. This is characteristic of tree sparrows, pipits, horned larks, snow buntings, and redpolls.

Perching birds offer the best opportunity to observe the distinctive characteristics and physical features of individual species. Flycatchers, for example, sit in a pronounced upright position—more vertical than similar species. By contrast, nighthawks and whip-poor-wills perch horizontally on a limb or wood fence; they have small weak feet, so they actually rest on their body feathers.

Birds in Shrubs and Trees

Notice the size and shape of the bill and tail (this is not at all difficult with a good binocular).

Seed-eating species, such as sparrows, finches, and buntings, have short, stubby bills.

The bills of cardinals and grosbeaks are thick and heavy, enabling them to hull and crack larger seeds.

The mandibles of the crossbills are actually crossed in scissorslike fashion. They are especially adapted to extracting seeds from the cones of our northern evergreens.

The woodpeckers have strong chisellike bills for "pecking" into wood.

Shrikes and sparrow hawks have hooked bills adapted to meat-tearing purposes.

Warblers and wrens have thin, sharply pointed bills for the purpose of catching small insects.

Not all birds "carry" or "hold" their tails in the same manner. Flycatchers have a tendency to droop or drop their tails below the angle of their bodies. Some, especially the phoebe, habitually flip their tails downward. Wrens cock their tails upward, often to a 45-degree angle or beyond.

Thrashers, mockingbirds, cuckoos, and grackles have long tails; the tail of the mourning dove is long and pointed.

Some birds—starlings, nuthatches, meadowlarks—have short, square tails. The tail of the mockingbird is rounded, the barn swallow's is forked, and the purple martin's is notched.

Certain species are expert tree climbers, notably woodpeckers, nuthatches, and creepers. The nuthatch is often seen coming down the trunk of a tree head first, giving it a unique advantage in spotting insects and grubs behind bits of bark that curl downward. The brown creeper invariably starts at the base of the trunk, clings close to the bark, uses its tail as a prop, and spirals its way upward. The woodpecker "hitches" its way up or down the tree; it also uses its stiff tail feathers as a supporting prop. The black and white warbler feeds in much the same manner as the brown creeper, but it hunts in either direction with equal facility.

Birds in the Air

The manner in which birds fly is one of the principal means of identification. The flight of some species is so distinctive that little else need be known in order to identify them.

Species such as robins, doves, cuckoos, and house sparrows fly in a straight line; woodpeckers, nuthatches, and goldfinches have a bounding or undulating flight.

Herons fly with a slow rhythmic beat; ducks must maintain a rapid wing beat for constant flight. Herons and bitterns fly with their long necks retracted, but ibises, storks, and cranes fly with their legs and necks fully extended.

Turkey vultures soar with their wings angled upward; the smaller black vultures and eagles soar with their wings much flatter—like a flying board.

Terns, kingfishers, ospreys, and sparrow hawks frequently hover in midair while hunting. Kingbirds, meadowlarks, and grasshopper sparrows have a fluttering style of flight.

The shapes of wings and tails are often distinctively outlined when birds are in flight, especially with the soaring varieties. It is one of the most helpful features in identifying the high-flying hawks.

Flight mannerisms and shape characteristics are also helpful in distinguishing families of similar-sized species, such as sparrows from warblers, and swifts from swallows.

The beaches and flats along the thousands of miles of our eastern coastline probably attract more birds in the course of a year than any other type of habitat. There is a special fascination in watching shore birds because they embody unique physical adaptations for survival in a great variety of biological conditions.

Herons, egrets, and bitterns are large, long-legged wading birds that stalk their prey. Their long, pointed bills are adapted to spearing fish, frogs, and aquatic insects.

Birds along the Shore

The roseate spoonbill is the most colorful of the long-legged waders. Its large spatulate bill is designed for sifting small fish, crustacea, and aquatic insects from the water and soft mud.

Among the smaller shore birds, dowitchers and sanderlings probe with their comparatively long bills, while plovers and turnstones pick at food on the surface. The turnstone's bill is curved slightly upward to aid in turning small stones, shells, and seaweed.

Avocets have long legs and long, upturned bills for the purpose of sweeping or skimming in the shallow waters of lake borders, flooded fields, and tidal pools; the black skimmer skims while on the wing.

Someone once said, "All ducks swim, but not all swimming birds are ducks." Other swimmers among our larger birds include swans, geese, brant, pelicans, gulls, cormorants, loons, grebes, anhingas, coots, and gallinules.

Birds in the Water

Because of light reflection and similarity in coloration, ducks and other "water birds" are frequently difficult to distinguish by color alone. Often, they can be most easily identified by their distinctive silhouettes, flight patterns, and field marks.

Each species of birds has a distinctive color pattern or physical feature that makes it distinguishable from other species. These prominent markings or features, known as field marks, include color patches, eye rings, wing bars, and the size and shape of bills, wings, tails, legs, and feet.

Using Field Marks

Field marks provide an effective means of distinguishing individual species within a family. The observer can determine by size and shape whether the bird in question is a hawk, heron, sparrow, or warbler, but beyond that point, other distinguishing features must be relied upon. In most cases, more than one feature, or field mark, is necessary for positive identification. For example, we cannot label the spring warbler we are watching as a Kentucky warbler just because it has an unstreaked yellow breast. If we check our field guides, we find there are a dozen other species that fit into this category, but the Kentucky warbler is the only one with black sideburns *and* yellow spectacles. Thus, the process of elimination, through comparisons, becomes an important factor in the use of field marks.

The beginning student will soon become aware of the fact that the most applicable combinations of field marks will vary according to families. For example, when we watch flying ducks, we are concerned primarily with wing and breast markings; with herons and egrets, the color of feet and legs is important; with terns, bills and caps must be considered. Five species of eastern thrushes are predominantly brown. They can be identified by the process of elimination—whether they have certain field marks or not. Rufous coloring, breast spots, eye rings, and cheek patches are the differentiating features. Warblers and sparrows are small and confusing, and a greater number of more specific field marks must be used. Here, we are concerned with such features as colorations, streaked or unstreaked breasts, wing bars, facial patches, eye rings, caps, and tail markings.

R. T. Peterson's *Field Guide to the Birds* is based primarily on the use of field marks. This method of systematizing the different visible features according to families, and the grouping of similar species within the families, is a most practical basis for the study and use of field marks as a means of identification. If you follow the Peterson system, you will become more adept at field identification as you become increasingly aware of *knowing what to look for*. For example, a sparrow lands on a bush in front of you; quickly, you note the breast is unstreaked, but that it does have a pronounced central spot. Instantaneously, you label it as a tree sparrow. The obvious question now is: How do I learn the field marks for so many species?

As in any learning situation, book knowledge becomes more meaningful, and is more easily retained, if accompanied by a means of practical application. If you know that tomorrow's trip will include a lot of bay ducks, some preliminary study of the field marks of the ducks you expect to see will be helpful. If you are going to the shore, study the sandpipers, terns, and other species you are likely to see along the beach. If you are planning a spring warbler hike, study the Peterson plates and accompanying text before you go. Once you actually see a bird as the book says it is supposed to be, you are likely to remember it on succeeding occasions. If you follow this practice— study the field marks of probable species before each field trip—you will be amazed at how the accumulated mental pictures will aid you in field recognition. Actually, it is unlikely that you will ever learn specific field marks for every species, but eventually you will know what to look for in each situation, and that is the key to being a good field observer.

Many beginning bird students learn to recognize birds by sight quite easily, but they often experience a mental block when it comes to identifying them by songs and calls. This should not be, for it is just as simple to recognize a bird by its song (unless you are totally tone deaf—and very few people are) as by its shape or color; sometimes it's much easier.

Learning Songs and Calls

The songs of birds are beautiful and exciting; they add much to the enjoyment of being outdoors. For the birder, their recognition is a must, for on most field trips (especially in the spring and summer) more birds are heard than seen.

I have taught many students to recognize birds by their songs and calls using the three steps that follow. If you are a beginner, or are having trouble learning and remembering bird songs, I recommend you give them a try.

Watch Birds Sing

This is probably the most helpful point of all: once you have positively identified the bird, *watch* it sing, and *listen.* As you listen, note its singing perch. Is it an exposed tree branch, or a utility wire? Is it a dead weed stem, or a fence post? *Watch* its singing attitude. Does it throw its head back and just let the song bubble forth, as the song sparrow does, or does it precede the song with some preliminary flutterings and contortions, such as the grasshopper sparrow frequently employs? Watching the bird sing—noting its singing perch and posture—will give you a mental picture that is easily recalled each time you hear that particular song. The song? The bird? It's an indigo bunting singing from the dead branch of a fencerow shrub!

Associations and Notations

We recall the name of a popular song by remembering the lyrics associated with that particular melody. Similarly, it is possible to recall the names of many birds by associating words with their songs. Of course, the easiest ones to remember are those that actually sing or call their own names such as the whip-poor-will, chuck-will's widow, bob-white, phoebe, wood pewee, and chickadee. Others are remembered by associating "sounds like" words or phrases with the songs. The examples given on the next page are more or less standards, and have been used by birders for many years. Their origin would be difficult to determine.

The use of words alone does not give you any indication as to whether one note is higher or lower than another, whether the notes are comparatively long or short, or which note or syllable should be accented. For this reason, you should develop a simple, personalized system of recording songs in your field notebook. As you associate words or syllables with a bird's song, you automatically memorize the rhythm; this becomes the basis for your notations. I use a simplified version of the system Aretas A. Saunders uses in *A Guide to Bird Songs.* The length of the note is indicated by the length of the line; the high or low quality of the note determines the line's comparative position. A wavering note or trill is indicated by a wavy line. Anyone interested in developing this system further should study Saunders's book.

For those of you who are musically talented (which I

Flycatcher, Least:	*"Che-beck."*
Ovenbird:	*"Teacher, teacher, teacher."*
Owl, Barred:	*"Who cooks for you?" or "Who cooks for you all?"*
Sparrow, Chipping:	*"Chip, chip, ip, ip, ipipippp."*
Sparrow, White-throated:	*"Ah, sweet Canada, Canada, Canada."*
Towhee, Rufous-sided:	*"Drink your tea," or "See towhee."*
Warbler, Black-throated Green:	*"Trees, trees, murmuring trees."*
Warbler, Chestnut-sided:	*"I want to see Miss Beecher."*
Yellowthroat:	*"Witchity, witchity witchity witch."*

definitely am not), Schuyler Mathews's *Field Book of Wild Birds and Their Music* may be of some help in developing a personalized system. I think it would be a decided advantage to be able to jot down a few musical notes along with your various symbols and words.

The important thing is to develop your own system— one that you understand. You will be surprised at how many "strange" calls you can record in the field with enough accuracy for future identification. Some calls, like those of the bobolink and winter wren, are virtually impossible to record with a pencil, but once identified they are not easily forgotten.

The actual voices of most North American songbirds have been recorded on a number of records and tapes. (See the Bibliography for a list and details.) The use of these recordings is one of the most effective ways of learning bird songs. They are especially helpful when selected calls (of birds most likely to be seen and heard) can be listened to prior to a field trip.

Recordings

There are two points I would make regarding the use of recordings:

First, the listener should have a visual picture of the bird doing the singing. It does little good to hear the song of a bobolink if you haven't any concept of its size, shape, or color. For this reason, recordings are most effective when used in conjunction with slides, pictures, or field guides.

Second, keep the volume down. I recall walking into an identification session and hearing a song sparrow screech and groan like a subway train pulling into a station. For the song to be recognizable in the field, present it as naturally as possible. If you have a large group, they will just have to listen—a good introduction to field-trip etiquette.

Of all the natural habitats in the eastern United States, the hardwood forest is by far the most extensive. Extending from the borders of Canada, where it is in a constant struggle for survival with its coniferous neighbors, it spreads a verdant summer carpet southward across mountain and valley until it fades into the subtropic vegetation of the Gulf states. It reaches westward until inadequate rainfall and excessive transpiration cause it to surrender to the dominant prairie grasslands. From its primeval vastness of nearly half a million square miles, we have carved our great metropolises, our towns, our highways, and our farmlands. Yet despite these intrusions by man, and lacking most of its pristine state, the deciduous forest dominates our eastern landscape.

This great, green carpet does not enshroud the land in its entirety with any singular hue or texture. Stained and blotched by the trampling of three hundred years of "progress," it struggles constantly to regain its pristine beauty and structure. In all degrees of growth, there is evidence that the forest seizes every opportunity to reclaim the land for its own.

In the southern Appalachians, this struggle ends in a climax forest dominated by the cucumber tree, beech, tulip poplar, sugar maple, white oak, buckeye, and hemlock. This is the geographical heart of this vast forest realm. It is the oldest exposed land mass of the region, and scientists believe a similar forest has existed here since

3 Birds of the Hardwoods

Tertiary times. It is also believed to be the center of origin for many of the widespread hardwood species. Here there is a great variety of trees, and the biological associations are quite complex. There are perhaps twenty or more species (in addition to those just mentioned above) that could be part of a climax condition.

In the northern portions of this mixed mesophytic forest, the beech and the sugar maple strive for supremacy. As the broken forest reaches westward into Wisconsin and Minnesota, the beech gradually gives way to the basswood. A large portion of our eastern coastal forests were dominated by an oak-chestnut association until the Asian chestnut blight made its appearance in New York City in 1904. Forests along the mountains from New England to Georgia were affected by this deadly disease. A variety of oaks, tulip poplar, and some hickory are the prevailing species today. Even in the hardwood's most southern range, the oaks (in different varieties and association) preempt the enduring forest. Mixed with them are the gum, ash, dogwood, hackberry, and a variety of shrubs.

This great American forest, enriched with ecological diversity, provides homes, food, and shelter for numerous endemic species of birds and wildlife. Even man seeks its sanctuary, for it is in these same middle latitudes—where the hardwood forest flourishes in all its richness and beauty—that man has clustered in the greatest numbers.

Quiet and subdued in the cold grasp of winter, the leafless trees stand bleak and lonely in a steel-gray world. The pulse of life is slowed, and all but the hardiest of creatures lie snug in the torpor of hibernation. But there are those who must defy winter's cruelties and keep the pulse of life astir. The fox plies his stealth in the silence of the darkest night. His coat is thick and warm; he does not mind the cold as long as he can satiate his hunger. The tiny shrew, voracious and bloodthirsty, must hunt almost continuously in order to survive. Neither day nor season gives him rest from his foraging. The cottontail rabbit and the white-tailed deer browse upon the tender shoots of young trees and shrubs—the forest must not be choked by its own lush growth. The staccato hammering of woodpeckers resounds from hill to hill; there are no leaves to buffer its

SOME NESTING BIRDS OF THE EASTERN HARDWOODS

Chickadees and Titmice,
    Chickadee, Black-capped
    Chickadee, Carolina
    Titmouse, tufted
Creepers,
    Brown
Crows and Jays,
    Crow, Common
    Jay, Blue
Flycatchers,
    Acadian
    Great Crested
    Pewee, Eastern Wood
Gnatcatchers,
    Blue-gray
Goatsuckers,
    Whip-poor-will
Grosbeaks,
    Rose-breasted

Grouse,
    Ruffed
Hawks,
    Broad-winged
    Red-shouldered
Nuthatches,
    White-breasted
Owls,
    Barred
    Great Horned
Tanagers,
    Scarlet
    Summer
Thrushes,
    Veery
    Wood
Vireos,
    Red-eyed
    Yellow-throated

Warblers,
    Black and White
    Cerulean
    Hooded
    Kentucky
    Ovenbird
    Redstart, American
    Worm-eating
Woodcocks,
    American
Woodpeckers,
    Downy
    Hairy
    Pileated
    Red-bellied
    Sapsucker, Yellow-bellied

resonance. Chickadees and nuthatches join them in their search for grubs and insect larvae. Visiting grosbeaks, finches, and siskins reap a harvest of late-clinging seeds.

Life within the winter woodland continues—now dormant, now active. Not until the wandering Earth exposes its northern latitudes to the more vertical rays of the warming sun will life resume its hastening pace.

The coming of spring is inevitable. Slowly at first, and then with a resurgence of life that fills the forest with the colors, the sounds, and the aromas of a newborn season, spring emerges.

In the low wetlands, the skunk cabbage and the marsh marigolds have thrust through the mucklike forest floor; the maples are tinged with red, and the spicebush spreads a yellow haze through the valley. The "kon-kor-reee" of the male red-wing can be heard along the stream's marshy borders. Higher on the ridge, the aspens are draped with fuzzy gray catkins. The ruffed grouse relishes them and welcomes the change in diet. The black and white warbler is there, too, searching the trees for the first hatch of insects. The first butterfly of spring, the mourning cloak, emerges from its winter cocoon and flashes its golden-edged wings. And the sweet smell of arbutus is wafted on the warming winds along the sunny hillside.

Now the flow of spring surges in every forest vein. The bloodroot and the hepatica are in bloom; May apples, wild columbine, Solomon's seal, and bellwort must make their maximum growth before the closing forest canopy deprives them of sufficient light. The fringe-loving dogwood wraps the forest in a tattered ribbon of white. The songs of birds resound from every level—the ovenbird from the forest floor, the wood thrush from his low perch, and the scarlet tanager from the highest tree. There are warblers and vireos, grosbeaks and orioles, flycatchers and buntings. The rushing tide of spring has reached its crest.

Spring: the season of flowers, songs, mating, birth, and growth—the season of life renewed!

Spring: the season that beckons the inherent traits of man—the season when those of us who are interested in birds must answer the woodland's call!

As you leave your car and the sterile ribbons of concrete behind you and step into the cool shade of the forest, you are entering the most dynamic of all outdoor communities. You walk down the trail, rest on a decaying log, and survey the green world about you. Everything you see, hear, touch, or smell is in some way involved in a life-building pyramid of ecological events necessary for the forest's survival. The birds you came to watch fill a significant niche in this mounting struggle for life's energy.

The square foot of soil beneath your feet is a compact mass of energy that is being produced, stored, and used simultaneously. Its tiniest creature, the soil bacterium, makes its bid for dominance by the simple and rapid procreation process of dividing itself into two complete individuals every half-hour or so. Biologists tell us that if all the offspring of one such bacterium survived, their bulk would be larger than the earth in less than a week. As the soil lives, the energy cycle of control evolves. Protozoa and fungi are the most abundant, but they are preyed upon the tides and the fury of ocean storms. Numerous bays extend inland, filling the valleys and lowlands, the paths of bygone glaciers. Southward from New England, the land slopes gradually into the sea. Actually, it can be looked upon as a huge delta extending from the mountains to the Atlantic, and then beyond to form the continental shelf. Here the mainland is protected by a series of outer beaches and long, narrow islands, built over the eons of mineral particles from the eroding mountains and carried there by the littoral current.

Over a period of years, I have had the opportunity to observe birds along much of our eastern coastline. I have seen the gannets dive in the Gulf of St. Lawrence. I have plied the foggy coast of Maine in the dory of a lobsterman, heard the fog horns growl, and seen the mirrored sun glow red on the morning's calm waters. I have roamed the beaches of Cape Cod, Long Island, Virginia, and the Carolinas. I have encircled Florida and the Keys, and felt the soothing warmth of Gulf waters on my aching feet. In the course of these ramblings, I reached some very positive conclusions concerning the watching of birds along the shore. I present them here, hoping they will temper your philosophy, enhance your enthusiasm, and make your seaside trips completely enjoyable.

• Most birding is more rewarding if done alone or with only a few companions. This is especially true along the beach. There are many other things to distract one's attention, and large groups have a tendency to string out along the way looking for shells, driftwood, etc. The area you want to watch becomes covered with people instead of birds.

• Early morning is best. The shore becomes "alive" as most creatures seek their first meal of the day.

• Expect the unexpected. Shore birding is unpredictable (one of its fascinations); the birds you expect to see may not be present, but they are often replaced by a rarity or two. The number and variety of birds present often depend upon the major movements of that particular day. This is especially true during spring migrations. Shore birds move north rapidly to take advantage of the short nesting season.

• Low tides expose larger feeding areas, and birds are

quick to take advantage of them. This is particularly noticeable in the North, where tide changes are greatest.

• Shore birds* often congregate around breakwaters, inlets, and brackish ponds. If birds are absent from the beach, these are the places to look for them.

• Late summer and early fall are the most rewarding times for watching shore birds. Cold weather comes early in the far North, and many species start south early.

• Fall plumages often are confusing. Carry a field guide, no matter how proficient in identification you may be. Often one or more birds will not conform to your memorized patterns.

• Colonies of ground-nesting birds should not be disturbed. Unprotected chicks are at the mercy of highly defensive and ruthless neighbors.

• Ocean storms frequently force rarities ashore. This is especially true during migration periods.

• A scope and tripod are an advantage at times, providing you have enough stamina to tote them. The scope is most useful in watching offshore birds, or for observing birds across bays and inlets.

• Dress warmly. The shore is usually cooler than you expect it to be. An unbroken ocean breeze can make the chill factor considerably cooler than inland temperatures.

• Carry your insect repellent. A fresh hatch of midges, or "no-see-ums," is like walking through a blizzard of tiny, hot ashes.

• The beach has more to offer than just birds. Observe its collections, life, and ecology. It will provide many excuses for additional trips.

• In summary: a low tide at dawn during August or September should be most rewarding.

There are differences between the rocky coasts and sandy beaches other than geological ones. Members of the marine phyla, and their relationships to one another, vary considerably. These ecological variances, in turn, attract those

---

* The term "shore birds," as used in this chapter, should not be interpreted in a technical sense as applying to waders only. It is used as a liberal collective term applying to all birds normally found along the shore, regardless of reason or scientific classification.

birds specifically adapted to significant roles in the completion of diverse patterns of life-chain correlations. The number and variety of birds found along the shore on any one occasion depend upon many physical and biological variables, especially during the seasons of migrations. The direction and intensity of the wind, for example, may account for large concentrations of shore birds, or for their complete absence. The significance of these variables has been taken into consideration in the preparation of the bird lists and text which follow.

Earth-shaping glaciers expended their awesome force at the edge of the sea some thousands of years ago. Stark, vertical cliffs, sculptured ledges, rounded boulders, and offshore islands stand as granite monuments to their passing, and to the land's gradual submergence into the sea. Now the sea is the dominant architectural force. With the unceasing wash of the waves, the rhythmic flow of the tides, and the surging violence of storms, it shapes its own boundaries.

Along the Rocky Coasts

The rocky coast is a picturesque area with a distinctive character of its own. It is moody, temperamental, and mysterious. Days can be clear and blue, bleak and gloomy, or wildly vicious. When an east wind blows the warm air from the Gulf Stream inward over the colder waters, an advection fog rolls in and shrouds the coast in an impenetrable blanket of gray. Fog horns moan their warnings, but boats and ships are harbor-bound. The "keouk—keouk" of a passing gull and the "wock" of a returning night heron come from somewhere within the depths of the thick, gray mist. Moisture drips from the coastal spruces festooned with the gray-green hangings of usnea; parula warblers build their basketlike nests within the entwining masses. The damp air aids the growth of algae and rock mosses, and they, too, become a part of life patterns along the shore. The engulfing shroud will persist until the breeze blows once again from the mainland.

Regardless of the weather, the sea rushes ashore with imperturbable consistency. It washes and splashes among the rocks and then recedes in curling designs of white foam. With it come countless numbers of marine life, some of which become entrapped in the washed-out basins, or tidal pools. There are microscopic forms, small sponges and worms, killifish, shrimp, jellyfish, limpets, periwinkles, and barnacles. Rockweed and Irish moss harbor matted colonies of minute bryozoan and shelter other aquatic creatures. Crabs crawl about the rocks, and beneath the shallow water there are starfish, sea urchins, mussels, clams, minnows, sea cucumbers, and a seemingly endless variety of wriggling life. The deeper waters teem with herring, cod, smelt, and other fish indigenous to the colder parts of the sea. Life is variable, and life is profuse. Otherwise, the great concentrations of birds along the rocky coast could not survive en masse. Enormous quantities of food must be available within the vicinity of an island that harbors thousands of birds in a single colony.

Yes, birds—thousands upon thousands of them—are irrevocably tied to the rock-bound coast and the adjoining sea. They must have their crustaceans, their mollusks, and their schools of herring, for the adaptations of time have so shaped their bodies and characterized their habits that they are akin only to the sea. Even man is captivated by the lore of these mysterious coastal waters; he must build his ships, follow the cod, trap the lobsters, and rake the clams.

Most of the great concentrations of birds supported by the bounteous waters of the rocky coast are to be found on the offshore islands—rocky promontories that were once a part of the mainland. To endeavor to list all the birds one might see on a trip along the coast and outer islands would be both precarious and presumptive, for this is an area of the unusual—the stragglers, the migratory wanderers, and storm-blown victims. With possibly two or three exceptions, the list on the next page includes those species which, in one way or another, are ecologically associated with the sea. No attempt has been made to include the woodland and grassland birds. Most of the following species nest during the early part of summer.

For bird watchers along our eastern coast, the gannets are surely the most entertaining and the most fascinating

Auks, Murres, and Puffins,
    Guillemot, Black
    Murre, Common
    Murre, Thick-billed
    Puffin, Common
    Razorbill
Cormorants,
    Double-crested
    Great
Gannets,
    Gannet

Gulls and Terns,
    Gull, Great Black-backed
    Gull, Herring
    Gull, Laughing
    Tern, Arctic
    Tern, Common
    Tern, Roseate
Herons,
    Great Blue
    Night Heron, Black-crowned

Ospreys,
    Osprey
Ravens,
    Common
Sandpipers,
    Spotted
Storm Petrels,
    Petrel, Leach's
Swallows,
    Cliff

of all the avian performers. Watching a large colony, such as the one on Bonaventure Island off the tip of Gaspé Peninsula, will challenge the full gamut of one's emotions, from sheer joy to utter sorrow. For the gannets themselves embody these traits and transmute them to the observer in moments of joyous flight and inherent ceremonial displays, in the terror of fitful panic, and, seemingly, through their own tragic stupidity.

In the air, the gannet is the personification of graceful flight. The sleek, streamlined body is a perfect airfoil, and it glides through the air silently, effortlessly, and with incredible speed. At times, the gannet flies just for the solitary exhilaration of flight. It will ride the updrafts of cliff-deterred air currents, hover on the lift of passing winds, or power-dive to near the water's surface. But mostly, the gannet patrols the coastal waters in search of a passing school of smelt, herring, or other fish. When a school is sighted, gannets gather and attack it en masse. From a predetermined height, sometimes as high as 100 feet or more, the gannets dive upon the school in a spectacular display of grace and agility. The dives are continuous, simultaneous, and often side by side, but they are skillfully controlled, and interference does not seem to be a problem. The dive is a fast, streamlined, arrowlike plunge into the school. The momentum of the dive will carry the gannet to the proper depth and help plane it upward beneath the school. The gannet captures the fish from below the school, as it returns to the surface.

On land, the gannet is a different bird; gracefulness and agility cease upon landing. In a manner bordering on comedy, it waddles and stumbles about, often to the consternation of its wing-tip-to-wing-tip neighbors. Courting ceremonies are diverse performances of dancing, bill clacking, gift exchanging, preening, and similar displays of affection. Should one bird suddenly panic, which it will sometimes do at the slightest provocation, the entire ledge may erupt in frenzied fright, knocking eggs and young into the sea. The gannet's normal method of departure from the high ledges is to hurl itself into space and plummet downward until it gains flying speed. This is a precarious maneuver for the young, and occasionally broken remains on the lower ledges attest to their misjudgment. But despite the gannets' specialized habits, and their pathetic tragedies, their numbers are increasing.

No other bird is so symbolic of the sea as the gull. Wherever one goes along our continental shores, there are always the gulls—"sea gulls," the collective term given to all members of the family by the uninformed, are everywhere. They follow our ships, congregate about harbors, and scavenge our beaches. But they are not of one species; they differ as do the herons, the swallows, and the sparrows. I have visited islands off the coast of Maine that have been dominated by great black-backed gulls, others by herring gulls, and on one occasion, a single island that held a small colony of laughing gulls determined to extend their range into the cold waters of the Northeast. Of these three species, the great black-backed is the most easily recognized and remembered, for its name implies both size and coloration. It is our largest gull and has a black back and black wings. The herring gull is the most common and often is used as a comparative basis for identifying other gulls (see page 138).

Your first trip to the offshore bird islands will be a surprising and memorable experience, but first, one thought of caution: Don't try it alone or with an inexperienced boatman. The tides rush between the islands in treacherous currents, and the fog can roll in quickly—an opaque curtain of white that can close behind you suddenly. Also, landing amid the rocks from a surging sea takes the right kind of boat and an experienced handler. If you contemplate such a trip, hire the services of a native, someone who knows the waters and the weather and has the proper equipment. It is also advisable to have a knowledgeable birder with you, because there are certain precautions that should be taken to protect the birds as well as the observer.

Islands dominated by nesting gulls seem to be places of constant alarm and confusion. There are screaming gulls in the air, on the ground, and in the water. If you should go ashore, the confusion becomes chaotic. Individual nesting territories are quite small and close together, and must be guarded almost constantly. The male usually does this from a favored rock or mound. Vegetation may be sparse, but the nest, or a portion of the defended territory, will be protected by the broken shadows of a clump of grass or weeds. This helps hide the young from overly zealous neighbors. Protective parents will not hesitate to kill trespassing young from an adjacent territory. The reaction is instinctive, and probably adds a sense of discipline to the colony. Select your travel route carefully—one that will cause a minimum of excitement among the nesting birds. Any extensive observations should be made from a blind.

Birds select a nesting island by its physical features and the availability of food. Whereas gulls prefer an island, or a portion thereof, with some shadowy cover, cormorants seem more secure in the open on high, rocky areas. An open island with a covering of sandy topsoil may appeal to the burrow-nesting Leach's petrel. The puffin also nests in burrows, but it prefers the crevices in craggy rock promontories. Similar areas are selected by the black guillemot—anywhere it can seclude its two eggs under a rock or in a crevice. The terns along the rocky coast will nest on mainland or island exposures of sand, gravel, or rocks, often in close association with gulls.

The cormorant can hardly be considered a beautiful or graceful bird. Surely, these attributes are nowhere in evidence about a nesting island. I recall visiting Old Hump Ledge off the coast of Damariscota, Maine, with the na-

tionally famed ornithologist Allan Cruickshank. Allan had warned the landing group that it was not a place for anyone with a squeamish stomach. The guano-covered ledge reeked with the acrid pungency of ammonia. In addition to the penetrating odor of the excrement, there was an unpleasant odor of fish—fish no longer fresh—some of which came from the regurgitated deposits of disturbed young cormorants. This, after a bounding ride in a small motor launch!

We also visited Matinicus Rock and observed a large colony of Arctic terns, a number of black guillemots, and the southernmost colony of common puffins on the Atlantic Coast. Puffins are more abundant along the coasts of New Brunswick, Nova Scotia, Newfoundland, and Labrador. Nesting puffins on Machias Seal Island, New Brunswick, for example, were estimated at 1,000 pairs for the 1971 season.*

The puffin is a clown. It is a short-necked, stocky bird that reminds one of a penguin, but the brightly colored facial makeup and the solemn dignity of its actions impart a reminder of circus comedy.

Things to look for while observing puffins include:

• Their tameness and calm dignity as you approach. This unsuspicious nature has undoubtedly contributed to their scarcity near populated areas.

• The exceptionally large, brightly colored, triangular bill. Outer portions of the bill are shed after nesting. Winter birds have smaller bills.

• The orange-red feet and legs.

• Only one egg per nest and one nest per year.

• Flight under water. The puffin literally "flies" through the water. This can be observed with binoculars, especially when the birds start their dive.

• Note the difficulty of a water takeoff in the absence of a strong wind.

• The landing. Whether on land or water, it is not particularly graceful—more of a stalled-out drop.

• Adults arriving at the nest with fish (usually capelin, a form of smelt). Although the adult may have a half-dozen

* Davis W. Finch, "Regional Report," *American Birds*, Vol. 25, No. 5 (Oct. 1971), p. 835.

fish in its large bill, observe the arrangement—perfect alignment, with tails on one side and heads on the other.

• An answer to a riddle often posed by Roger Tory Peterson: "How can it hold onto the slippery fish while adding another to its collection?"

Most any trip along the rocky coast or amid the offshore islands will undoubtedly add birds, other than those already mentioned, to your daily list. Murres and razorbills may be spotted about the cliffs, and a raven may be seen scavenging along the water's edge. Cliff swallows sometimes find an overhanging ledge to their liking and will nest in large colonies. Spotted sandpipers rear their young along the gravelly beaches of open, grassy islands. And perhaps a Wilson's petrel, escaping the cold winter of its Antarctic breeding grounds, will wing its way across your bow. Also, you will find that each isolated area has an ecology of its own. An inquisitive approach to the differences and to the relationships will bring you rewards more exciting than mere bird recognition.

Along the Sandy Beaches in Summer

Grain by grain, the sand comes and goes along our beaches —millions of tons of it every year. The long, sandy shoreline is not a stable boundary; it is constantly in the process of changing—now building, now receding—at the whimsical mercy of the winds and the waves, by the dreaded force of storms, and by the incessant power of ocean currents. Through these forces, over the centuries, extensive barrier islands, or outer beaches, have built up along our eastern seaboard. The barriers protect the mainland from the full fury of these same awesome forces.

As the sand builds along the shore, much of it is carried beyond the normal tide line during periods of storms and exceptionally high tides. This process builds the inner, or middle, beaches. When the sand dries, it is carried farther inland by the wind until it is dropped or deterred by protruding vegetation. In some places, and over long periods of time, such action is sufficient to build high sand dunes. These dunes may be stabilized by pioneering beach-grass and succeeding vegetation, or they may creep inland, as sand is lifted off the windward side and dropped on the leeward, or inland, side. Bayberry, high-tide bush, poison ivy, and other coastal plants become established as sufficient humus is added to the sand by decay and wind. Birds play a pioneering role through seed distribution, excrement deposits, and nesting activities. Cottonwoods and pines may become established and prepare the soil for succeeding oaks. Eventually, the soil may become rich and moist enough for beeches and maples to become dominant. At each level, and at each stage, the bird life will change.

Along the water's edge, the moisture-soaked beach abounds with such life as sand hoppers (beach fleas), mole shrimps, and sand-collar snails. Sanderlings, sandpipers, plovers, and other shore birds pick and probe about the wet sand in search of these small marine creatures. At the highest reach of the tide, a drift line forms along the beach. Sea weeds, an occasional dead fish or bird, and assorted debris accumulate until disturbed by an even higher tide. Flies, beetles, and other insects swarm about the decaying debris and provide an additional source of food for birds that follow the shore. Life is relatively sparse on the dry inner beaches, but becomes abundant again in the line of coastal vegetation. Many spring and fall transients from other habitats can be found here, including swallows, warblers, hawks, thrushes, and flycatchers. The offshore waters teem with floating and swimming organisms. From the myriad of tiny, single-celled plant diatoms, microscopic protozoa and other minute crustacea, through swimming mollusks, minnows, and larger fish, a dynamic life chain energizes the sea and furnishes sustenance for the diving birds.

During the nesting season, one often is surprised by the small variety of birds to be found along the ocean beach. There are reasons for this. First, and perhaps the most decisive, is the lack of cover required by most nesting species. The offshore waters do not contain the abundance of larger plant and animal forms as found in the waters along the rocky coast, so the life chains are more specialized. Also, many of the shore birds, which are so numerous along the beaches during spring and fall migrations, nest

COMMON SUMMER BIRDS OF THE SANDY BEACHES

Gulls and Terns,
  Gull, Great Black-backed
  Gull, Herring
  Gull, Laughing
  Tern, Caspian
  Tern, Common

Tern, Least
Tern, Royal
Oystercatchers,
  American
Plovers,
  Piping

Wilson's
Sandpipers,
  Willet
Skimmers,
  Black

in northern interior regions. However, there are birds, such as gulls, terns, and black skimmers, that nest in great colonies on protected beaches.

At one time or another, a majority of our eastern birds can be found along the beaches, or in the vicinity of adjoining coastal waters and vegetation. An endeavor to list them all could hardly produce accurate results. The list at the top of this page contains only those species closely associated with the beaches during the nesting season. Migratory and wintering birds are covered elsewhere in this chapter, and the tropical species are included in the following chapter.

In addition to the nesting species, other birds often can be observed along the beaches during the summer months. Herons and egrets come to the water's edge to feed; grackles and crows forage along the drift line. You may see a hunting sparrow hawk, or get a glimpse of one of the coastal sparrows in the adjoining grasses. The shore holds the element of surprise at any season.

Terns are likely to be the first, and often the most common, birds you will see when visiting the beach during the summer. They are very active and excitable birds, mostly white with black caps, pointed wings, and forked swallow-like tails that have earned them the collective name of "sea swallow." You will see them hovering and then suddenly dive head first into the water after their favorite prey. The terns fit into the shore's ecological pattern by feeding mostly on a variety of small minnows.

With few exceptions, terns nest in sizable colonies. This

TERNS ASSOCIATED WITH EASTERN BEACHES

CASPIAN TERN

Identifying field marks: Nearly gull-sized, but has a black cap, a heavy blood-red bill, and a forked tail.

Range: Breeds in scattered colonies, both along the coast and inland, from Canada south to the Gulf Coast.

Nest: Coastal birds prefer the security of offshore islands. The nests are mere depressions in the sand and shell fragments. Seaweed and grass are sometimes used to line or shape the nest.

Food: Dives for fish like other terns, but often feeds from the surface in a gull-like manner. Also, it has some of the gulls' predacious habits, and has been known to rob nests of eggs and small birds.

Habits: The Caspian often is referred to as "the king of the terns," and rightly so. It is the largest and most aggressive of the terns; it is also less gregarious and more independent than other members of the family. Often associates with the ring-billed gull.

COMMON TERN

Identifying field marks: Orange-red bill with black tip.

Range: The most widely distributed tern. In the East, from Canada south to around Florida and the Gulf states. Also abundant along the larger inland lakes.

Nest: Prefers open sand or gravel beaches of offshore islands, or isolated sections of the main shoreline. The nest may be just a slight depression in the sand or pebbles, or it may have a skimpy lining of grass or seaweed.

Food: Mostly small fish such as the pipe fish, sand launce, and the fry of alewives, menhaden, and other coastal species. In some sections, small crustacea form a substantial part of their diet.

Habits: Dainty and graceful in flight. Often follows schools of feeding mackerel, bluefish, or striped bass to feed on the scraps and crippled minnows left in the wake of these voracious feeders.

LEAST TERN

Identifying field marks: Our smallest tern. White patch between the bill and black cap. Yellow bill.

Range: On the coast, from Massachusetts south to Texas. Also breeds along main inland river systems.

Nest: Favorite coastal sites are extensive sandy points that reach out into the sea. A small hollow in the sand and bits of broken shells; contains two or three buff-colored, brown-spotted eggs, which match their surroundings.

Food: Small fish, a few crustaceans, and aquatic insects obtained mostly by diving.

Habits: Excitable, noisy, but harmless to other species. Often nests in the same localities and in harmony with piping plovers and Wilson's plovers.

ROYAL TERN

Identifying field marks:	*A large tern. Long, slim, orange bill. Black cap ends in tufted crest. Deeply forked tail. Wings extend beyond tail when perched. Often confused with Caspian tern.*
Range:	*Breeds from Virginia along the coast to Texas. Wanders as far north as New Jersey in the summer.*
Nest:	*Nests in very compact colonies on sandy offshore islands. Two tan, brown-spotted eggs are laid in a slight depression in the sand.*
Food:	*Small fish caught by diving, or by following surface schools, and quickly dipping into the water for individual fish.*
Habits:	*Feeds mostly in offshore ocean waters. Nesting birds are so close together they almost touch. One wonders how they can find their own nests repeatedly.*

gives them the advantage of mutual protection, and concentrates the nesting period for all pairs into a minimum length of time. But this dense concentration of nesting sites is sometimes a disadvantage to the species as a whole. Their habit of nesting on comparatively low sand and gravel beaches makes the entire colony vulnerable to ocean storms and exceptionally high tides. If you approach a nesting colony, you will be subject to the diving attack of screaming, irate birds, the same reception given to any intruder. The smack of a wing, the scrape of a foot, or a peck from a sharp bill at one's head should be sufficient warning to deter further intrusion. Actually, colonies should not be disturbed. Exposed eggs will bake in the excessive heat of the sun and be subject to predation by gulls, crows, rats, and even ants.

The species of terns most closely associated with our eastern beaches are the Caspian, common, least, and royal. A brief account of each is given in the table opposite and above.

At times, the shore seems to belong to the gulls alone. They patrol the water's edge, feed from the surface, and are ever on the alert for a free handout from a passing boat or a surf fisherman. They are garrulous, noisy, and quarrelsome. The harsh, defiant screams of the great black-backed and herring gulls are heard from the Arctic south to Long Island and northern New Jersey. The laughing gull maintains a slim and precarious hold along the New England coast, but it is basically a warm-water bird. Its hysterical laughter of "ha-ha-ha" is a common sound along the southern Atlantic and Gulf coasts. Coastal islands with grass and other low vegetation are favored as nesting sites. The small size, black head, solid dark mantle, and white trailing edge of the wings distinguish it from the two preceding species.

Special adaptations to the unique and varied ecological niches of the coastal waters are exemplified by the black skimmer and the American oystercatcher. In each case, the bill is adapted, and almost limited, to feeding in a specific manner. Such specialization limits competition for preferred foods.

The black skimmer is a comparatively large, slim, black and white bird with a wingspread of more than 3 feet. The bill is most diagnostic; it is long, bright red, and tipped with black. It appears to be quite heavy, but actually it is compressed flat and thin vertically. The lower mandible is nearly a third longer than the upper one. The skimmer has been known by many colloquial, but apt, names such as cutwater, scissorbill, sea crow, and sea dog. Cutwater is undoubtedly the most appropriate name of all, for it implies the manner in which the bird feeds. It does not skim, but flies low over the water, cutting the surface with its long, thin, lower mandible. When a fish or shrimp is touched, the upper mandible snaps shut like a trap, pulling the bird's head back beneath the body.

The skimmer feeds mostly in the early morning or late evening hours, when small school fish are nearest the surface. If you watch it feed, you will notice that it cuts the water in a long, straight line, reverses itself, and follows the same line in the opposite direction. There is considerable conjecture among ornithologists as to whether the repeated traversing of the same general line attracts feeding fish to the surface, thus making capture easier. From personal observations of skimmers feeding in the canal adjacent to my backyard, I believe this to be true. I have watched individual birds feeding continuously for 10 minutes, and as they traversed back and forth lengthwise of the canal, their feeding lines were no more than 6 inches apart, even though the canal is more than 60 feet wide.

The American oystercatcher is a large spectacular bird of the shore. The contrasting black and white plumage, long, red, chisel-shaped bill, and pinkish legs are the best identifying features. It feeds mainly on oysters, clams, mussels, snails, and other crustaceans. When exposed bivalves open their shells, the oystercatcher inserts its strong chisel-bill and severs the muscle that holds the shells together. The contents are then helpless and easily obtained.

Both the skimmer and the oystercatcher seek the security of offshore islands for nesting, their nests being mere "scrapes" in the sand. They are most abundant on selected islands from Virginia southward, and along the Gulf coast to Texas. Loud and garrulous, their presence adds an audible charm to the shoreline that is as characteristically significant as the defiant call of the gull or the excited cry of the tern. Peterson describes the black skimmer as "yelping like a small lost dog." The call of the oystercatcher is a sharp, piercing, and oft-repeated whistle of "wheep-wheep-wheep."

But not all birds of the shore are involved in the raucous melee of the nesting season. The piping plover, sand-colored and inconspicuous, goes about the business of rearing its family in a quiet, unhurried manner. As we watch this pale "ringed" bird feeding along the water's edge, it reminds us of a robin feeding on our lawn. It patters ahead, stops, cocks its head slightly to the side, and watches for some morsel of marine life. Insects, larvae, marine worms, small crustaceans, and tiny mollusks are the main items of food. The piping plover's soft, plaintive call of "peep-lo" does not emulate the hysteria of its neighbors.

Another "ringed" plover, the Wilson's, is found along our eastern beaches. Not as common as the piping, it can be recognized by its larger size and proportionately large, heavy, all-black bill. The call is also distinctive—an emphatically whistled "queep, queep." Both species nest amid the sparse grass of sandy offshore islands. The piping plover